ON THE MARKET

by

Jason Odell Williams

Uproar Theatrics

LICENSING & PRODUCTION INQUIRIES
Uproar Theatrics, LLC.
hello@uproartheatrics.com | www.UproarTheatrics.com

CHARACTERS
(4 actors with doubling, or up to 21 actors without doubling)

CHARLOTTE - white female, 40s-50s. Jewish American, raised in Israel. (No accent.)

DIANE - female, 40s-50s, any race.

FRANK - male, 40-50s, any race.

JAMES - male, 40s-50s, any race.

Suggested doubling breakdown when using four actors:

- DIANE also plays Eccentric Wife, Rustic Wife, Excited Girlfriend and Nice Wife.

- FRANK also plays Date #2, Date #4, Eccentric Husband, Chatty Husband 1, Rustic Husband, and Nice Husband.

- JAMES also plays Grief Counselor, Date #1, Date #3, Mark, Chatty Husband 2, Excited Boyfriend, and Delivery Guy.

SETTING
Present Day. The suburbs of Long Island.

ON THE MARKET had its world premiere on Oct 15, 2022 in a production by CenterStage Theatre at the JCC in Rochester, NY (Ralph Meranto, Producing Artistic Director). Directed by Donald Brenner the cast was as follows:

Charlotte	Beth Winslow
Frank (and Others)	D. Scott Adams
Diane (and Others)	Esther Winter
James (and Others)	John Winter

NOTES:

The pace of this play is fast and bright! Think *Gilmore Girls* or *The Marvelous Mrs. Maisel*. It's peppy, witty banter... until they're forced to slow down during the sweeter moments, but they don't slow down for too long, or in too many places. These characters tend to fight against the grief and heartache by powering through with humor.

The play's running time is ideally around 80 minutes.

Capitalization of words that would not ordinarily be capitalized (like when Charlotte says, *"we all want our surviving spouse to Pine Endlessly"*) are simply clues for the actors to give certain words a little something extra. It's not italicized indicating weight, or in quotes indicating irony, but rather Capitalized to indicate a Slight Lift. Do with that what you will. ;-)

Slash marks (//) denote a point of overlap between one speaker's line and the next speaker's line.

Text in brackets *[...]* should be implied but not said out loud.

Like Charlotte, the characters of Diane, Frank and James are real and grounded, while still being upbeat and funny. The "other" characters can be broad and over-the-top. Go big! Have fun!

The set should resemble a tasteful home for sale that's decorated "to show." Ideally it's a small compact space, with the rooms all flowing and butting right against one another. There can be a kitchen/dining area, an office area, a living room area, and an outdoor patio. Or it can be one generic all-purpose space: more abstract than literal. Each space can be used practically or representationally. There do not need to be walls or doors, but there can be practical pieces like a sofa, a kitchen island, desks and chairs in the office, etc. Do what's best for the space you're in!

Transitions are meant to be fast and seamless. Entrances and exits should dovetail, overlap, and be anticipated with little to no dead air between scenes.

<u>TIMELINE FOR JAMES</u>:
He was diagnosed around three and a half years before the play begins, then died a year later (29 months before the play begins).

PROLOGUE

> *Cheesy game show music plays as lights snap on revealing CHARLOTTE in a pool of light down center. She's holding a long, thin microphone and a typed letter. She looks at them both in her hands, confused as...*

> *Lights snap on revealing DIANE down stage right, also holding a long, thin microphone. She gestures vaguely to a "house" behind her, delivering her lines like a game show host.*

DIANE

On the market for 23 weeks, this 67-year old Cape Cod style home has a living room with a painted-brick fireplace, a formal dining room with a bay window, and a newly renovated stone patio on one half-acre. Listed at six-hundred-ninety thousand!

> *Diane gives a cheesy smile and turns toward FRANK as lights rise on him standing down left. He gestures vaguely to a "house" behind him.*

> *He also sounds like a cheesy game show host and has a long, thin game show style mic.*

FRANK

On the market for 35 weeks, this 59-year-old split-level ranch style home with hardwood floors, a living room with a gas fireplace, and a gorgeously situated backyard pool is listed at just five-hundred-eighty thousand!

> *Frank and Diane look at Charlotte who snaps into game show host mode, but looks as if she's being possessed, like something is <u>making</u> her say and do these strange things.*

CHARLOTTE

New to market, this 45-year-old* widow with Danish
interiors and a hard Israeli exterior comes with a crippling
fear of the unknown, a lovely daughter attending a college I
can't afford, plus a dog who pukes in car rides over ten
minutes! All this can be yours for the low-low price of
simply... *(game show music cuts out)* having a steady job and
not being a total douche-nozzle.

> *NOTE: The age said here can be altered to suit
> the actress.*

> *Charlotte tilts her head with a smile as the game
> show music finishes: buh-buh-buh-BUH-bump!*

> *Frank and Diane exit as...*

SCENE: GRIEF COUNSELOR

> *Lights shift revealing a GRIEF COUNSELOR
> sitting in a chair/sofa, wearing glasses and a
> cardigan sweater. He's a bit pretentious, a lot of
> nodding with his hands pressed together near
> his chin. He speaks with an accent (Irish,
> Scottish or British).*

GRIEF COUNSELOR

And the dream always starts the same?

CHARLOTTE

Exactly the same.

> *Charlotte moves to the area where the
> Counselor is. She can sit near him or pace in*

front of him as she talks.

CHARLOTTE

I'm holding a poem that James wrote on that old-timey typewriter he used to have...?

GRIEF COUNSELOR

Interesting.

CHARLOTTE

But I can't read it, the words are all blurry and fuzzy.

GRIEF COUNSELOR

Interesting.

CHARLOTTE

And that's when I *usually* wake up, but last night in the dream suddenly Diane and Frank were there!

The Counselor opens his mouth to say something but Charlotte cuts him off.

CHARLOTTE

Diane's my best friend since forever and Frank works with us both at the realty office. Super nice guy. Really funny. Total mench.

The Counselor nods/shrugs as if to say: "Not what I was gonna ask, but proceed."

CHARLOTTE

Anyway, we're all on the set of some cheesy game show, shilling houses behind "Curtain Number One" or whatever -- but it also felt like I was selling *myself*...? Like on a dating website or something?

GRIEF COUNSELOR

Interesting.

CHARLOTTE

...You say that a lot, ya know.

GRIEF COUNSELOR

Do I? ...Interesting.

CHARLOTTE

Yeah, you should work on that.

> *The Counselor looks a touch offended, but Charlotte doesn't notice/doesn't care and carries on.*

CHARLOTTE

Anyway - the dream's a *sign*, right? I mean, it has to be! Like *(like an old Rabbi) WHY IS THIS NIGHT DIFFERENT FROM ALL OTHER NIGHTS? (normal voice)* Because I've been going on all these *dates* recently and my dead husband isn't happy about it, so he's sending messages while I sleep, telling me to pump the breaks.

GRIEF COUNSELOR

Well, I would argue // that the dream --

CHARLOTTE

You would argue that the dream is my subconscious telling me the recent dates were real progress - I'm putting myself "on the market" so to speak - which is healthy. Right?

GRIEF COUNSELOR

Exactly.

CHARLOTTE

Well. Agree to disagree, Counselor.

GRIEF COUNSELOR

I'm a "grief counselor," not a lawyer--

CHARLOTTE

Yeah, yeah, yeah, I'd love to stay and chat, my guy, but don't wanna dip into "golden time," so...

She starts out.

GRIEF COUNSELOR

Wait--

She stops.

CHARLOTTE

I know what you're gonna say.

GRIEF COUNSELOR	CHARLOTTE
There's no clock on grief.	There's no clock on grief.

CHARLOTTE

Uh-huh. Some people need a few months, others a few years.
Anger, bargaining, depression, acceptance. Any one of those
stages would be a step forward after losing James. But I've
been talking to you for over two years now, and somehow
I'm _still_ in denial. That about cover it?

> *He's about to say something when _a soft bell_*
> *_dings_.*

CHARLOTTE

Annnnd that's the hour. *(She takes a quick, cleansing*
breath.) This was good - real progress, I think. Same time
next week?

> *Lights shift.*

SCENE: AFTER-WORK DRINKS

> *Charlotte moves to a small outdoor table at a*
> *cafe as Diane and Frank approach. Diane has a*
> *glass of white wine.Frank has a glass of white*
> *wine and a beer. He hands the wine to Charlotte.*

FRANK

Sorry. They were out of rosé.

DIANE

Can you believe it? *(Yelling behind her)* What kind of
restaurant runs out of rosé?

| CHARLOTTE | FRANK |
| If it has alcohol in it, I'm fine. | If it has alcohol in it, she's fine. |

CHARLOTTE

Ha, jinx! *(Raises her glass)* L'Chiam!

FRANK

Cheers.

Frank and Charlotte start to drink.

DIANE

Wait-wait-wait, I wanna make a toast.

They stop sipping. (Maybe Frank spits his beer back into the bottle??)

DIANE

Okay first: To my two favorite employees.

FRANK

Your *only* two employees.

DIANE

Which makes you my favorite.

CHARLOTTE

Wouldn't that also make us your least favorite?

Frank chuckles, Charlotte smiles.

DIANE

Hey Abbot and Costello, would ya lemme finish - I'm trying
to compliment you!

CHARLOTTE
(cheeky)
Oh, then please, by all
means!

FRANK
(equally cheeky, Cockney
accent)
Very sorry, mum, won't
happen again.

DIANE
(ignoring their goofy banter)
And a special toast to... Long Island's hottest realtor for her
most recent sale! Whoop- whoop!

FRANK

Definitely the hottest realtor.

They look at Frank.

FRANK

I meant "hot" like on a winning streak, not sexy or attractive.
(Backpedaling) Not that you're NOT those things, I just
mean... *(Cheesy announcer voice)* "Selling that split-level
ranch style home with a gorgeously situated backyard pool!"
That was hot.

Charlotte snaps a surprised look at Frank.

CHARLOTTE

Wait - why did you say that?

FRANK

Sorry. Trying to explain the "hot" thing - but I'm an idiot, I'll stop--

CHARLOTTE

No, no - I mean, why did you say it like *that* - in that funny announcer voice?

FRANK

Oh. Just goofing around. Isn't that, like... our thing?

CHARLOTTE
(slightly weirded out)
...Huh.

DIANE

Anyway - congrats, gorgeous! Three sales in two weeks. You're closing deals like they're going outta style.

FRANK

Yeah! She's a closing *machine*. Gonna start calling you Mo Rivera.

CHARLOTTE

Who?

FRANK

Mariano Rivera. Old relief pitcher for the Yankees? *The greatest closer ever*?!

CHARLOTTE

I understood, like, *three* of those words.

FRANK
(jovial)
Right - I forgot. James wasn't a "sports guy."

DIANE
(not cool)
Hey.

FRANK
Oh sorry. Charlotte, I, I, I-- // didn't mean to--

CHARLOTTE
No, no, it's fine, you're right. James was not a sports guy. He preferred to occupy his day with things that actually mattered.

FRANK
Touché.

CHARLOTTE
And you guys _can_ talk about him around me. I actually _like_ it. He died, but that doesn't mean he didn't exist.

> Small awkward beat. Frank sips his drink. Diane
> gives Charlotte a sympathetic smile, then...

DIANE
(all business)
Okay - moving on. Any progress on the dating front?

CHARLOTTE   FRANK
Oh, God. No. Please.   Here we go…

CHARLOTTE
(to Frank)
She cares more about my love life than her own marriage.

DIANE
Come on! You went out with that friend of your cousin's last night. How was it?

CHARLOTTE
Awful, horrendous, atrocious. What's another word for terrible -- oh yeah, IT SUCKED!

Frank chuckles.

DIANE
It couldn't have been *that* bad.

CHARLOTTE
The guy last night thought women should *not* have the right to vote. And the guy last week had a neck tattoo... of his ex-wife's breasts!

Frank and Diane take in that image. Then Frank slowly raises his hand with a question.

FRANK
...How big were they?

Charlotte puffs out a laugh. Diane gives Frank a look, maybe swats his arm, not amused.

CHARLOTTE
(to Diane)
Look: I gave it a shot, but clearly dating is NOT in the cards for me right now.

DIANE

That's 'cause you're dating pool is too small. You need to expand into the _online_ world.

CHARLOTTE

No way - I'm still pissed you talked me into filling out that stupid profile to begin with.

FRANK

Agreed. Online dating is the worst.

CHARLOTTE

I mean, what guy's gonna be interested in a middle-aged widow with bad knees and insomnia.

DIANE

Please. You're a total catch.

CHARLOTTE

Nope. // Not buyin' it.

DIANE

Come on. Frank - you're a guy. Isn't Charlotte a total catch?

FRANK
(embarrassed)

Yeah. Of course. Total - total catch.

DIANE

See?

CHARLOTTE
(to Frank)

We work together. You have to say that.

FRANK

No, even if we didn't. I mean, like _objectively_. *(Sincere)*
You're smart, pretty, really funny. A genuinely kind person.
Anyone would be lucky call you their wife or... girlfriend.

CHARLOTTE
(genuinely touched)

Aw, thank you, Frank. But enough about me. Diane - how
are the kids. Does Ruby still want to be a marine biologist?

DIANE
(sing-song)

You're deflecting again.

CHARLOTTE
(sing-song)

'Cause I don't wanna talk about me dating again.

DIANE

It's been two and a half years.

CHARLOTTE

No - it's only been 29 months.

DIANE

Isn't that the same thing?

FRANK

Two years is 24 months, plus another half year, would be 30
months.

CHARLOTTE

See.

                              DIANE

It's been a _long_ friggin' time, okay! And James would have
wanted you to move on by now.

                            CHARLOTTE

You know - people _say_ that. But I'm not so sure. I mean yes,
he and I talked about how this day would eventually come,
and he said all the right things, _"I want you to be happy, to
Find Love Again."_ But I looked in his eyes, and I gotta tell
ya. He didn't mean it.

                Frank chuckles, knows Charlotte is being funny.

                              DIANE

Char.

                            CHARLOTTE

No - deep down, I actually think we all want our surviving
spouse to Pine Endlessly and never find love again. Just --
schhhhooop! (_She makes a trap-door closing sound, then
switches to a polite Flight Attendant Voice_) "Sorry,
passengers - this Vagina is Closed. Please try a younger, less
jaded one."

                              FRANK
                     (standing, but also laughing)
        Annnnd that's my cue.

                              DIANE

See? You scared off Frank. Talking about closed vaginas.

                            CHARLOTTE

Oh! I'm sorry, Frank, stay. No more vag-talk, I promise.

14

FRANK

No, no. You're fine. But I also know when I'm a third wheel, so.

CHARLOTTE

You're never a third wheel.

FRANK

It's cool, I uh... got some stuff to do around the house anyway. You two have a great night, and uh... *(fancy actor voice)* I shall bid you both adieu!

He does a dorky salute / bow. Crickets.

FRANK

...I don't know why I did that. See ya Monday.

Frank dashes out. Charlotte chuckles. Diane shakes her head, "Frank is weird."

CHARLOTTE	DIANE
Bye, Frank. Have a good weekend.	Drive safe!

Frank exits.

DIANE

Okay - what's really going on? You're seriously "going out of business forever?"

CHARLOTTE

No, it's just... I know how everyone _thinks_ this is supposed
to go: *(rattling it off like a headline)* Grieving Widow Picks
Up the Pieces, Finds Love a Second Time, blah, blah, puke.
But maybe I'm an outlier! Maybe James was my One and
Only -- and I should be grateful for what we had.

DIANE

I'm not saying Be Ungrateful, // I'm just--

CHARLOTTE

You _know_ that I still dream about him. I mean, if that's not a
sign--

DIANE

Not everything is a sign.

CHARLOTTE

Hey! You watched that Netflix doc with me -- about ghostly
encounters and the afterlife? You said you believed that stuff
could be real.

DIANE

We had two bottles of wine - I believed Bigfoot was real.

CHARLOTTE

So don't you think these dreams could be James trying to tell
me something?

DIANE

The only thing James would be trying to tell you is to Move
On and Be Happy.

CHARLOTTE

I *am* happy. Imogen is doing amazing at NYU, I have a great job with great friends, a sweet dog, and subscriptions to Netflix, Hulu, Amazon, Peacock and a new one called "Never-Leave-Your-House-Again PLUS." Life is good.

DIANE

And having someone to *share* it with could make it even better.

CHARLOTTE

Or worse.

DIANE
(here we go again)

Oh, god.

CHARLOTTE

Seriously. I watch "Dateline!" So many second marriages end up with the husband frantically calling 911 after a freak boating accident! No - I think the real takeaway here is: don't get on a boat with a second husband.

DIANE

Okay - I was hoping you'd come to your senses by now, but I've also known you since The Macarena was invented, so... *(pulls out her phone)* I went on Match-dot-com and set up a few dates for you.

CHARLOTTE

Wh--?! Can you even *do* that?

DIANE

I created your account, I have all the passwords.

CHARLOTTE
(scoffs)

[Unbelievable!]

DIANE
I did you proud. Trust me.

CHARLOTTE
You <u>*covertly*</u> set up dates and I'm supposed to <u>*trust*</u> you?!

DIANE
Look - I'm not expecting miracles. None of these guys are
gonna be Mr. Right.

CHARLOTTE
Then what's the point? I already had the two worst dates
since Eva Braun met Adolf.

DIANE
It's a process! You don't hop on a thoroughbred right outta
the gate. You need a few "old mares" and ponies before you
get back in the saddle.

CHARLOTTE
Hey, Hopalong Cassidy. Comparing the dates I had to
horses...

CHARLOTTE	DIANE
is an insult to horses.	Is an insult to horses. Uh-huh.

DIANE
This is happening - all right? You're going on these dates or
I'm divorcing us as best friends.

CHARLOTTE
(sighs)
...Fine. But the "Best Friend Divorce" threat is gettin' a little old.

DIANE
(looking at her phone)
If it ain't broke.

CHARLOTTE
...So. When is this first "magical rendezvous?"

DIANE
(looking at her phone)
Oh. Right now.

CHARLOTTE
Now?! Are you kidding?!

DIANE
(standing, excusing herself)
Nope - here he comes. Sit up straight. And, uh... don't forget to smile!

CHARLOTTE
Wh-- Diane -- *(hushed, angry)* Diane!

Lights shift.

SCENE: MATCH-DOT-NOPE

*Charlotte stays in her spot as Diane moves
upstage (still holding her glass of wine) to*

*oversee the action. Diane can't be seen or heard
by the dates - only by Charlotte.*

DIANE
(full-saleswoman mode)
This one is a real... "diamond in the rough."

*DATE #1 enters. He wears a backwards
baseball hat and has a toothpick in his mouth.
Sits backwards on a chair facing Charlotte.*

DATE #1
'Sup, gorgeous. I'm Tommy. But you... can call me... Mr.
Wonderful.

CHARLOTTE
...Ew.

An "incorrect answer" buzzer sounds.

*Date #1 leaves and is immediately replaced by
DATE #2. Think Steve Urkel meets Sheldon from
"The Big Bang Theory."*

DIANE
A fixer upper with lots of potential.

DATE #2
Hi, Charlotte, lovely to meet you. I'm Saul.

CHARLOTTE
Nice to meet you. (*Gestures to her glass of wine*) Would
you... like a drink?

DATE #2

Sure. Nothing with alcohol though. Or dairy. Or nuts. Or high-fructose corn syrup. Or food coloring. Or a plastic straw. The planet is dying, I can lift the glass to my own mouth, thank you very much.

He laughs a very weird laugh at his own joke.

CHARLOTTE
(to an unseen waiter)

Can we get some _water_ over here? (*Loud whispers)* And the _check_?

Buzzer sound. Date #2 exits as DATE #3 sweeps on holding an elaborate fruit-filled cocktail.

He's already crying.

DIANE

Needs some TLC...?

DATE #3
(crying)

And then she said she'd _call_ me. But she never called me! What's _wrong_ with me?

CHARLOTTE

Nothing! You seem like a... really sweet guy, Brad.

DATE #3

It's _Chad!_

CHARLOTTE

Oh, right, well. You're gonna make someone _very_ lucky one day. Chad.

DATE #3

...You mean that person isn't _you?!_

CHARLOTTE

Ooo. Buddy. Did you think this was going well?

> _Charlotte makes a face like, it's not going well._
> _Date #3 CRIES LOUDER!_

> _Buzzer sound. Date #3 leaves and is quickly_
> _replaced by DATE #4 (who speaks with an_
> _Australian accent) holding a beer. He's a decent_
> _guy with potential._

DIANE
(fingers crossed)

Solid bones on this one....

> _Diane exits, hopeful._

DATE #4

So she moved back to Melbourne. I kept the house. But we
never had kids, so. If ever a divorce can be clean...

CHARLOTTE

Yeah. It almost sounds sweet.

DATE #4

I loved her, ya know. You can't negate that. We just wanted
different things as we grew older. It happens. Anyway -
enough about me. Your profile said you're a realtor?

CHARLOTTE

Yeah. Just a fancy word for Real Estate Agent. It's not my calling in life, I wanted to be a singer, but... it pays the bills. For now. And college is expensive, so.

DATE #4

Ah! You go to uni?

CHARLOTTE

No - my daughter. She just started at NYU this year.

DATE #4
(his interest suddenly wanes)
Oh, wow. And, uh *(searching for something polite to ask, but doesn't really care)* What's she studying?

CHARLOTTE

Everything. Nothing. Who knows. She talks about becoming an actress. Or a psychiatrist. Or a public school teacher. So -- she'll probably be a lawyer.

> *Charlotte chuckles. He half-smiles. She's charmed. Finally a date is going well!*

CHARLOTTE

Hey, do you wanna get some appetizers? The mozzarella sticks are really good here.

DATE #4

Oh. I would but. (*Sucks his teeth.*)

CHARLOTTE

They hurt your teeth...?

DATE #4

Appetizers usually mean you _like_ me and maybe things would progress, but you seem really nice, so I'm just gonna level with you. I don't date women with kids.

CHARLOTTE

...I see.

DATE #4

I just never understood 'em to tell the truth.

CHARLOTTE

Kids - or women _with_ kids?

DATE #4
(plowing on)

They're loud and expensive and their hands are always sticky with food.

CHARLOTTE

Well my kid's 18, so if her hands are sticky, it's probably not food.

DATE #4

...You should probably change your profile - mention you have a daughter. Some guys would be totally into that - divorced _dads_ and whatnot.

CHARLOTTE

But not you.

DATE #4

Sorry. (_Points to himself_) Old dog.

CHARLOTTE

"No new tricks." Got it.

Charlotte stands to leave.

DATE #4

But hey, if you want... we can still have sex.

CHARLOTTE

Aw, no thanks. I don't wanna get my hands sticky.

She gives him an ironic smile.

A long buzzer sound indicates the end of the "game." Date #4 leaves as Diane reenters with her glass of wine.

Lights shift.

SCENE: IT'S A SIGN

Diane sits next to Charlotte.

DIANE

So, we're oh-for-four. Big whoop. This was a warm-up anyway.

CHARLOTTE

No, this was another sign.

DIANE

We don't believe in signs.

CHARLOTTE
You. _You_ don't believe in signs. I am a firm devotee of the
Universe Is Telling Me Something doctrine. And right now,
the Universe is _screaming_ at me, loud and clear: _(cups hands
together to yell)_ "Stop dating randos off the Internet." _(talks
normal)_ Stop dating _period_!

DIANE
You really think the Universe with all the crap it has to
worry about is taking time to send you signs about your love
life?

CHARLOTTE
I do. So - thanks for your concern. But I'm out.

Charlotte stands to go. Diane grabs her arm.

DIANE
Wait - Char. Please...

CHARLOTTE
What.

DIANE
James was the best. Great husband, incredible father, and
one of the most talented builders in town.

CHARLOTTE
Agreed. What's your point?

DIANE
I just -- I understood a mourning period. A period of
reflection and regrouping. Time to get Imogen off to college.
But... it's been two and a half years. _(Charlotte is about to
correct her but Diane cuts her off)_ Almost! ...And you're still
not yourself.

26

CHARLOTTE
My husband died - okay. I'll _never_ be myself.

DIANE
// I know.

CHARLOTTE
So I'm sorry if my "recovery" isn't going according to whatever _schedule_ you have in mind...

DIANE
// I never said that.

CHARLOTTE
But I'm doing the best I can. I'm mostly off Ambien, I don't cry for 20 minutes straight anymore...

DIANE
Yeah, 'cause you don't cry at _all_ anymore. You don't feel _anything_ anymore.

CHARLOTTE
Tsh.

DIANE
Seriously. Other than Cranky or Snarky, you haven't had a genuine emotion in months!

CHARLOTTE
I'm an Israeli Jew -- Cranky and Snarky are our official mascots!

DIANE
...I rest my case.

CHARLOTTE

So - what - I should start crying at dumb rom-coms - will
that get you off my back?

DIANE

Maybe! Or get back to singing? Like you used to! At least
for fun. But I don't think you're capable of that. Not until
you open your heart.

CHARLOTTE
(standing to go)
Okay, Deepak Chopra. I'll keep that in mind. What do I owe
ya for the drinks?

Charlotte opens her purse to get some cash.

DIANE

Nothing - don't // worry about it.

CHARLOTTE

Oh, oh! And I forgot to show you this!

*She pulls out an old Post-it note from her purse
and hands it to Diane.*

DIANE

What is this, what am I looking at?

CHARLOTTE

That. Is the last note my husband ever wrote to me. Read it.

DIANE
(reading note)
"Broken." ... What's broken?

CHARLOTTE
...Well, originally it was about our treadmill that wasn't working - the note must've fallen off at some point. But while I was cleaning out the garage yesterday, do you know how I found it again? *Stuck*. *To the bottom*. *Of my shoe*!

DIANE
...So?

CHARLOTTE
So?! It's a literal sign. From my husband!

DIANE
About a broken treadmill!

CHARLOTTE
(getting emotional)
ABOUT ME! As in: *I'm* broken.

DIANE
Oh. Babe - you can't really think that.

CHARLOTTE
Well, it doesn't matter 'cause I do. So thanks for trying, but... I already used my heart once. Perfectly. And I can't bear to have it broken again.

> *Charlotte exits, forgetting the Post-It that Diane still holds.*
>
> *Diane sighs. She looks at the note, thinking. Lights shift.*

<u>SCENE: THE LETTER</u>

> *Charlotte re-enters and crosses into a pool of*

light. She takes a beat to gather herself, then
puts on a cheerful smile.

CHARLOTTE

This twenty-one hundred square foot ranch-style home with
a newly renovated solarium, a home office with built-in
bookshelves, and a meddling best friend who won't leave her
alone is wondering if this is really what the rest of her life is
going to be like after six weeks on the market   It also has a
garage!

An ECCENTRIC COUPLE enters looking
around the space. (As the name implies they are
eccentric. Feel free to play them big, bold and
weird. Think Aidy Bryant and Bowen Yang on
SNL.)

ECCENTRIC HUSBAND

It's niiiiice.

ECCENTRIC WIFE

Veeeeery nice.

ECCENTRIC HUSBAND

The renovations are *particularly* nice.

ECCENTRIC WIFE

Agreed. It's all... very very very very nice! (*to Charlotte*)
Who did the renovations - do you know?

CHARLOTTE

Uh. They were actually done by my late husband's
company... Dennison Builders?

ECCENTRIC HUSBAND

Indeeeeeed - they're one of the best outfits on Long Island.

ECCENTRIC WIFE

Indeed indeed indeeeeeeeeed.

Charlotte nods, maybe bites her lip trying not to laugh at this very odd couple.

ECCENTRIC WIFE

And thank you again for letting us in early.

ECCENTRIC HUSBAND

Yes! We were driving by and saw the sign, *(really loud)* "OPEN HOUSE - TODAY AT TWO!!" ... *(normal)* but we have the Hershkovitz bar mitzvah at two.

ECCENTRIC WIFE

And you can't be late to a bar mitzvah. Otherwise you'll end up at the _back_ of the buffet. All the _lox_ will be gone!

CHARLOTTE

It's no problem. I was just about to get set up anyway, so. Happy to oblige.

ECCENTRIC HUSBAND

Do you have any paperwork on the renovations? When was it completed, did it pass inspection, so on and so forth.

CHARLOTTE

I do, yeah - just a sec.

While the couple continues to look around, Charlotte digs through her shoulder bag and pulls out comp fliers, a sign in sheet, then an accordion folder with a flap cover and elastic cord closure.

CHARLOTTE

Sorry, I'm not completely organized yet.

ECCENTRIC WIFE

It's our fault entirely! *We made you open up before you were ready.*

ECCENTRIC HUSBAND

I told you she wouldn't be ready!

CHARLOTTE

No, you're good. It's just - I usually look over all the paperwork ahead of time. But I haven't reviewed this one for a while. It was on the market over three years ago - then the owners loved the renovations so much, they ended up keeping it, so.

ECCENTRIC WIFE

Oh! Like "Love it or List it!" We love that show. *(to her husband)* Don't we love that show?!

ECCENTRIC HUSBAND
(poking around the walls)

We love-love-LOVE that show. So these renovations are three years old? They look brand new.

ECCENTRIC WIFE

BRAND NEW!

CHARLOTTE
(looking through accordion folder)

Well, like I said. My husband and his team did great work. Ah. Here we are.

She pulls out a stack of papers and hands them to the Husband.

ECCENTRIC HUSBAND
Mm, yes, thank you. *(Quickly flipping through, he finds something out of place)* Whoops. Looks like a personal letter got slipped in with the rest.

*He hands Charlotte **a small envelope** with her name __typed__ on the cover. Charlotte is confused and intrigued.*

CHARLOTTE
Oh. That's weird. But thank you. So! What do we think of the house?

Charlotte stares at the letter again, transfixed.

ECCENTRIC HUSBAND
It's niiiiice.

ECCENTRIC WIFE
Veeeeery nice.

ECCENTRIC HUSBAND
But I'm not super keen about a primary bedroom on the first floor.

ECCENTRIC WIFE
True-true. *(to Charlotte)* Do you have anything with a more traditional layout? ...Hellooooo?

CHARLOTTE
(in a flurry, ushering them out)
Sorry - this is the only listing I have right now, win some-
lose some, you can show yourselves out - tell the bar
mitzvah boy "Mazel Tov" for me.

ECCENTRIC WIFE
...Well, that wasn't very nice.

*The Eccentric Couple exits as Charlotte moves
downstage, staring at the envelope.*

*She takes a steadying breath... then rips open the
envelope and reads the letter inside.*

JAMES appears upstage, reciting the note.

JAMES
*"We were each other's soulmate; that kind of
love is rare. And the cards that we were dealt...
may often seem unfair. But while it's hard to
hear, the conclusion is foregone.*

What you need most, Dear Charlotte...

JAMES	CHARLOTTE
... is to Move On. "	... "is to Move On.

Charlotte looks up.

Lights shift.

SCENE: MIRACLE OF MIRACLES

*At the office, Charlotte shows the letter to Frank
and Diane.*

DIANE
It was just sitting in the listing folder?

CHARLOTTE
(nodding)
Uh-huh. And see how it's typed on an old-fashioned
typewriter - exactly like his 1933 Smith Corona!

DIANE
Right! For his poetry stuff.

CHARLOTTE
So I think James left this note to help me... find my next
great love.

DIANE   FRANK
Oh my God.   ...Whoa

Beat. They all soak that in.

DIANE
That... is so romantic!

CHARLOTTE
Isn't it?!

*She and Diane squeal & giggle. Frank sort of
smiles along but also seems suddenly nervous
(though he hides it well).*

DIANE
(to Frank)
Isn't this amazing, Frank?

FRANK

Yeah, no - totally wild. I'm just... precessing ya know, taking it all in.

CHARLOTTE

Frank thinks I'm crazy.

FRANK

No, not at all, I just --

CHARLOTTE

You're thinking, "how'd the note even get there without being found until now?"

FRANK

Actually no, but now that // you mention it--

CHARLOTTE

So, clearly a _ghost_ didn't type this letter "from the great beyond." James wrote it once he knew the cancer was aggressive. Then he put it with the renovation certificates thinking I'd find it once the house went on the market -- _after_ he'd died. He had no idea the owners would see the final product and change their mind about selling. So I never looked at any of this paperwork till today!

FRANK

Wow, that's. Wow.

CHARLOTTE

I know, right? Anyway - I got another listing - but I wanted you both to see this first.

DIANE

Amazing, sweetie! The miracle of miracles. We're so happy
for you. *(Blowing air kisses)* Mwah, mwah, mwah!!

CHARLOTTE

Thanks. See ya tomorrow.

DIANE

Byyyyyeee.

Charlotte leaves. Diane immediately spins to face Frank.

DIANE

Okay, Debbie Downer. What gives?

FRANK

Nothing. Whaddya mean. I'm happy for her.

DIANE

...Yeah, you seem thrilled.

FRANK

What - you want me doin' backflips 'cause she found some
note telling her to move on? Please. It's no big deal.

DIANE

...Ohhh my god! ...You're acting weird because you like her
again!

FRANK

"Again?" What do you mean "again?" We've always liked
each other here, all three of us. It's a friendly office.

                    DIANE

Dude. Come on. I knew about your little "crush" when she
first started. It was kinda cute.

                    FRANK

I never had a crush.

                    DIANE

Laughing at all her jokes? Showing her around the office??

                    FRANK

I wanted her to understand how the printer works. It's very
finicky.

                    DIANE

I can't believe you like her again! When did this happen?

                    FRANK

Never! I don't like Charlotte. Well. I mean - yes, I "like"
Charlotte, she's a good friend and a great colleague, and
really smart and attractive and a wonderful human being
who always smells like lilacs and springtime but I don't like
her in that way.

                    DIANE
                    (sweet)
Oh, Frankie. What're we gonna do with you?

                    FRANK

Nothing. There's nothing to do, 'cause I don't like her, so --
(He looks at Diane. She's not buying it.) Please don't say
anything.

DIANE

…Okay. Oo! How 'bout this! I won't set her up on any more dates so the field can remain open just for you.

FRANK

For me? No. No no // no no no no no

DIANE

Come on! Why not?

FRANK

Because it's weird. And _I'm_ weird. Plus we work together, so it would be weird and never work out and... did I mention I'm _weird?_

DIANE

Frank...

FRANK

Just - please. Let it go. For me?

DIANE
(sighs)
...For what it's worth, I think you two would make a great couple. Even _James_ would approve.

FRANK

That's nice, but it doesn't matter 'cause it's never gonna happen.

DIANE

Maybe. Maybe not. But I do agree with you about _one_ thing.

FRANK

What's that?

DIANE

You're friggin' weird.

>*She sticks out her tongue then smiles. Lights*
>*shift. Diane and Frank exit.*

SCENE: MEETING MARK

>*Charlotte stands in a pool of light.*

CHARLOTTE

This post-war fixer-upper with sudden naive optimism --
thanks in no small part to her dead husband's final romantic
gesture -- comes with a fragile heart, infinite potential, and a
wood-burning fireplace. Eight weeks on the market.

>*She moves into the space to show it to a nice-*
>*looking man, MARK. He speaks with a charming*
>*Southern accent.*
>
>*While Charlotte is cordial with him, she's not*
>*super outgoing like she usually is. Her mind is*
>*elsewhere.*

MARK

It's big.

CHARLOTTE

Nice open concept, yeah.

MARK

Seems like a fair price, too.

CHARLOTTE
Priced to move, as they say.

MARK
(knocks on a wall)
Solid bones.

CHARLOTTE
They don't make 'em like this anymore.

MARK
You wanna have dinner with me?

CHARLOTTE
Once in a lifeti-- what?

MARK
I, uh. Asked if you wanted to have dinner. With me. Some time.

CHARLOTTE
...I'm confused.

MARK
Sorry. I'm terrible at this. I've been divorced a little over a year and recently all my friends have been trying to get me to go on these... dating websites. Have you heard of these? Awful, soul-sucking, anxiety-inducing, Crimes-Against-Humanity. Anyway, to get 'em off my back, I had to promise I'd at least _try_ to put myself out there - but it always felt so forced. And I never really go out or meet new people. But you are without a doubt the nicest, smartest, most attractive woman I've met in a while who isn't 26 or a struggling Model-slash-Actress or both... and also not wearing a wedding ring. So. No pressure. You can absolutely say "no" - but at least this way I can tell my friends I "Put Myself Out

MARK (cont)

There." So to speak.

Pause.

CHARLOTTE

You like Thai food?

MARK

I love Thai food.

Lights shift.

SCENE: FIVE DATES IN FIVE DAYS

Charlotte is at work with Diane and Frank.

CHARLOTTE

His name is Mark, he's a film and TV editor, divorced with two grown kids -- and he can
cook.

DIANE

He cooked for you already?

CHARLOTTE

We've already had five dates, so. He cooked on date number three.

DIANE

But you met him on Sunday.

CHARLOTTE

I know.

                    DIANE
Today's Friday.

                    CHARLOTTE
I know!

                    DIANE
You had five dates in five days?

                    CHARLOTTE
I had five dates in five days!

*Charlotte nods while smiling like a goofball and does a little
"happy dance."*

                    DIANE
I gotta say, I am liking this new Charlotte.

                    CHARLOTTE
Me too! And it's all because of that note. That magical note.
It just... *freed* me. Guiding and encouraging me to move on.
And oh! I didn't even tell you the weirdest part.
Mark...? Kinda *looks* like James.

                    DIANE
Really? How similar we talking? You got a picture?

                    CHARLOTTE
Yeah, here. *(Opens her cell phone)* See? ... Kinda like if
James wore cowboy boots and sounded like Blake Shelton.

            *Diane takes the phone. Frank peeks over
            Diane's shoulder to see Mark's photo.*

DIANE
Wow, okay! Yeah, I can see it.

CHARLOTTE
So you don't think it's weird that the first guy I seem interested in looks exactly like my dead husband?

DIANE
It just means you have a type. If my husband died, as much as I'd like to think I'd marry Idris Elba next... I know I'd end up with Keenan Thompson. I like 'em soft and non-threatening.

CHARLOTTE
You're right, you're right. I'm overthinking it. *(Looks at watch)* And I gotta a listing in twenty minutes, yikes. *(She gathers her stuff)* Call you later?

DIANE
You know I'm always here for ya. Got nothing else going on in my life!

Diane laughs a little too hard at her own joke.

CHARLOTTE
…Uh-huh Okay byyyyeeeee.

DIANE
Byyyyyeeeeee.

Charlotte exits. Frank spins to face Diane.

FRANK
You gotta tell her to dump Mark!

                         DIANE

Whoa, easy there, bud.

                         FRANK

I'm serious. She'll listen to you.

                         DIANE

Look, I know you wanted to ask her out yourself, // and you
still can --

                         FRANK

No - that's not why. You just - you gotta tell her to break up
with him.

                         DIANE

And why would she do that? Mark sounds like a great guy.
Any woman would be lucky to have him.

                         FRANK

Plenty of them already have!

                         DIANE

...What?

                         FRANK

Mark...? Is "Open House Guy."

                         DIANE

...I don't know what that means.

                         FRANK

Okay, he's this guy I've seen at a few open houses. Never
makes an offer on anything. Just there just there to pick up
women.

DIANE

At an open house?

FRANK

I'm telling you. He hits on realtors, single moms, divorcées, any woman with a *pulse!* He's like the Wedding Crashers of Open Houses. He's an Open-Crasher!

DIANE

You sure it's the same guy?

FRANK

Positive.

DIANE

...*Or*... is this just you trying to break them up so you can swoop in and be her knight in shining armor.

FRANK

I'm not swooping! I hate swooping, I never swoop! But this guy's a total sleaze-ball, I'm telling you.

DIANE

I don't know, man. You saw his picture for like two seconds and now you wanna rain on her parade, tell her the first guy she actually likes since her husband died is some Open House Crasher?

FRANK

I'm not raining on anything // I'm just--

DIANE

Come on! We all know the reason you've never settled down is because of your obsession with Charlotte.

FRANK

I don't have // an obsession--

DIANE

So either tell her how you feel -- finally! -- see if she chooses you. Or butt out. But telling her about Mark...? Only hurts Charlotte.

Diane exits. Frank is alone. Lights shift.

SCENE: GRIEF COUNSELOR

Charlotte sits on a sofa across from the Grief Counselor. (He still speaks with an Irish, Scottish or British accent.)

GRIEF COUNSELOR

Sounds like you're making some good progress.

CHARLOTTE

Definitely. I mean, who says you need to go through all five stages of grief? Maybe you just sort of get over them all at once and boom! Back to your old self.

GRIEF COUNSELOR

Well, I would...

GRIEF COUNSELOR
caution about moving too
quickly.

CHARLOTTE
Caution about moving too
quickly?

CHARLOTTE

Please, I am crushing these stages. I mean, sure I was sad,
had some rough days there in the beginning--

GRIEF COUNSELOR

Like when you didn't get out of bed for two weeks.

CHARLOTTE
(a touch annoyed)

LIKE I SAID... some rough days in the beginning. But now
I'm feeling good, exercising again. Seeing this great new
guy.

GRIEF COUNSELOR

That doesn't mean you can *ignore* your loss --

CHARLOTTE

Or maybe I just Won at Grief. Ever think of that?

GRIEF COUNSELOR

Grief isn't something you win.

CHARLOTTE

Why not? People talk about Beating Cancer all the time.
Why not Beating Grief... after *losing* someone to cancer!!

*The Counselor opens his mouth to reply when
the bell dings. Time's up.*

CHARLOTTE

Uhp! ...To be continued.

Lights shift.

SCENE: TILL THERE WAS YOU

> *Late afternoon at the office, Frank and Diane*
> *work in silence. It's a bit awkward.*

> *Finally, Frank turns to Diane.*

FRANK
...Hey, do you have that new listing comp?

> *Diane finds the paper he needs and slaps it*
> *down on the desk in front of him without a word.*

FRANK
Are we still doing the "not talking to me" thing?

DIANE
I don't know, Frank. Are you still planning on breaking my best friend's heart?

FRANK
I'm not breaking anything, I'm just telling her the truth about that guy!

FRANK	DIANE
Isn't that a good thing? Being honest? Not keeping secrets?	Not everybody wants to hear the truth. 'Cause it doesn't make anyone feel better but the person telling it!!

> *Charlotte enters. They get quiet.*

CHARLOTTE

...Why do I feel like I just walked in on Mom and Dad fighting?

DIANE

No! We're good. Good good good. Right, Frankie?

FRANK

Right... Diane-y. All good in da hood.

CHARLOTTE

…Weird.

FRANK

....So listen, Charlotte. // I wanted to tell you something--

DIANE

Uhp uhp uhp howwww was your open house, how'd it go? Any offers, nibbles - what's new, pussycat - whoa-whoa-whoa!

CHARLOTTE

...Okay seriously what's going on? Are you guys having an affair?

DIANE
Ew. No. Gross. Not that Frank is gross. He's just like a brother to me. That's why. But no. Nothing nefarious here. Nope.

FRANK
No, no, no, no. That's not. I have far too much respect for Diane _AND_ the sanctity of marriage. So. Nope. Nada happ'nin' 'round here, partner.

FRANK

...But speaking of nefarious, I wanted to tell you som--

Diane <u>tackles</u> (or pushes) Frank to the ground!

CHARLOTTE

...OH MY GOD! WHAT IS WRONG WITH YOU GUYS?!!

They get up, each dusting themselves off.

DIANE

Nothing! Nothing. Just jokin' around *<u>Right</u>? <u>Frank</u>?*

FRANK

Yeah. Yeah, just joking.

CHARLOTTE

Okay...?

FRANK
(super fast)

Except Mark crashes Open Houses to pick up women and I have proof he's been lying to you.

Diane hangs her head. Damnit!

CHARLOTTE

...Wh--? Are you guys still messing with me?

DIANE

Haha! Yes. Gotcha. April Fool's!

CHARLOTTE

It's October.

DIANE

...That's what makes it so funny??

CHARLOTTE

Seriously. _What_ is going on.

> Beat. Frank looks at Diane. She gestures to him,
> "Go ahead, tell her."

FRANK

So that guy Mark? He came to an open house of mine a few
months ago.

CHARLOTTE

And...

FRANK

And I heard him talking to the other realtor, Lisa, about
being divorced and how his friends have been trying to get
him on the dating apps, then finally he said to her _(bad
version of Mark's Southern accent)_ "but you are without a
doubt the nicest, smartest, most attractive woman I've met
who isn't 26 or a struggling Model-slash-Actress or both."

CHARLOTTE

...What?!

FRANK

And I've seen him do the same thing at a few Open Houses
since. Including one this morning. I took a photo Ignore the
bagels in the foreground.

_He shows Charlotte his phone. She looks at the photo of
Mark hitting on a woman. It sinks in._

CHARLOTTE
(to Diane)
…You knew about this?

DIANE
No! I mean, only after Frank told me.

CHARLOTTE
When did he tell you?

DIANE
...Yesterday?

CHARLOTTE
And you only thought to tell me now? And you barely
seemed like you wanted to tell me at all!

DIANE
Only because I knew how upset you'd be. I was trying to
protect you.

CHARLOTTE
I don't need your protection.

DIANE
Of course not. I meant help. Guidance. You were just starting
to put yourself out there after you got that letter, so I thought
you could use even _more_ help from me, that's all.

> *Oops. Did Diane just say the quiet part out
> loud? She tries to play it cool, but Charlotte
> (and even Frank) can sense something's up.*

CHARLOTTE
...More help from you? Like with the website and setting up
dates, you mean?

DIANE
Yeah. The site. And the dates. That's all.

Something dawns on Charlotte.

CHARLOTTE
Diane.

DIANE
What.

CHARLOTTE
Don't make me say it.

DIANE
Say what?

CHARLOTTE
...Did you write that letter from James? Diane?

Silence. Frank looks at Diane, stunned.

CHARLOTTE	DIANE
Diane!	YES! I wrote it, I wrote the letter.

CHARLOTTE
…Wh– how?

DIANE
It doesn't matter --

CHARLOTTE

How?!

DIANE

I tried things the old-fashioned way, all right. Giving you
advice, setting you up on dates. But you weren't having it.
So... I gave you a little nudge.

CHARLOTTE

A nudge?

DIANE

A push.

FRANK
(mutters)

A "shove" is more like it.

DIANE

Hey. It wasn't some big diabolical plan. It just happened! I
was browsing on Etsy, looking for a fun shower gift for my
niece - found this great t-shirt that says _"I Need a MOM-osa.
Like a mimosa only Stronger!"_ Isn't that just perfect?

> _Diane snort/chuckles. Charlotte is not amused._
> _Frank shakes his head "no." Diane drops her_
> _smile, immediately pressing on._

DIANE

Anyway, I randomly came across a typewriter _exactly_ like
the one James had... and I knew it was a sign.

CHARLOTTE

You don't believe in signs.

DIANE

Everyone believes in signs, we just don't admit it! Anyway, you were showing me that old Post-it about your "heart" being broken and since you weren't listening to my advice but you _were_ listening to old notes from James... I bought the typewriter and wrote you a note - just to speed up the process of you getting out there. _I thought I was helping!_

CHARLOTTE

No one asked for your help!

DIANE

That's what makes it so nice - I did it without asking!

CHARLOTTE

You see?! _This_ is why I didn't want to go on any of those dates. It always leads to _This_!

DIANE

// Babe, come on.

CHARLOTTE

Messy feelings and disappointment and _resenting_ my best friend who seems weirdly _obsessed_ with my love life!

DIANE

That's absurd. // I'm just concerned about --

CHARLOTTE

I was completely content drinking wine and watching old episodes of "Friends." Because Ross and Rachel...? They never let you down.

FRANK

Very true.

CHARLOTTE

But you - my best friend in the whole world - you let me down.

DIANE

Please. Ross and Rachel were constantly letting each other down - the whole show was about their screwed up relationship!

CHARLOTTE

But it always worked out in the end 'cause the other friends _helped_! It's right there in the theme song: (*fast, angry - maybe even angry singing*) "I'll Be There For You!" Because they all cared more about each _other_ than _themselves_!

DIANE

I _care_ about you! I barely see my husband and kids anymore 'cause I'm sneaking off to set up dates and write notes --

DIANE	CHARLOTTE
Hiding them in the listing folders without you catching me.	Can you hear yourself?! ...You sound crazy!

FRANK	CHARLOTTE
Hey, okay, maybe we should turn down the temperature a notch, huh?	You have _completely_ crossed the line and and and and...

CHARLOTTE

... I don't know if I can _work_ here anymore!

DIANE

...You don't mean that.

CHARLOTTE

I do! ...But I also still need this job, so... why don't we pause our friendship and you can go back to your dull, unfulfilling life.

DIANE

What's that supposed to mean.

CHARLOTTE

It means I can't be the replacement for your family who doesn't need you anymore.

> *Diane scoffs, maybe turns away, not wanting to hear more but Charlotte digs the knife in deeper. Frank stays out of the way.*

CHARLOTTE

Your life revolved around your kids but now they're older and don't need you as much, and your husband's always traveling for work, which makes you feel lonely and unimportant, so you stick your nose in _my_ business. Well here's some advice: Stop using me as an excuse to avoid your own life! And butt out of mine!

> *Hurt, Diane exits. After a long beat. Frank steps*

back toward Charlotte.

FRANK
(trying to break the tension)
...I totally agree about Ross and Rachel, by the way, they were the heart of the show.... Sorry, too soon?

CHARLOTTE
...What do *you* think I should do?

FRANK
About...?

CHARLOTTE
My life. Dating. All of it.

FRANK
Oh. Doesn't matter what I think.

CHARLOTTE
Sure, it does. We've known each other almost ten years. I value your opinion.

FRANK
Over ten actually.

CHARLOTTE
Really?

FRANK
You started here ten years ago this past March. So ten years and seven months.

CHARLOTTE
Wow. See? You're smart *and* have a great memory. So... what do you think I should do?

FRANK

I don't know... do what makes you happy.

CHARLOTTE
(buzzer sound)
Ennnnnh! Sorry, bud - got a ruling from the Judges and that's a totally weak answer, we're gonna need ya to // tell us what you really–

FRANK
I THINK YOU SHOULD GO OUT WITH ME!

CHARLOTTE
...think.

Silence.

FRANK
...I'm gonna sit down. I didn't realize how much it would take out me, saying that out loud.

CHARLOTTE
Yeah. Let's both sit.

They sit on the floor, maybe their backs against the side of a desk. They look at each other, then look away.

FRANK
Sorry. I shouldn't have said anything. Now it's just weird.

CHARLOTTE
No, no. Good to get that kind of thing off your chest. Get acid reflux otherwise.

FRANK

(touching his chest, slight discomfort) That could explain the recent heartburn.

Small beat.

CHARLOTTE

...How long have you...?

FRANK

Had heartburn?

CHARLOTTE

Had feelings. For me.

FRANK

Oh, let's see... you started working here on March 15th ten years ago, I remember because you made a joke about the Ides of March and hoping you didn't get stabbed in the back on your first day.

CHARLOTTE

There's that killer memory.

FRANK

So I probably started have feelings for you arooounnnd... March 16th?

CHARLOTTE

As in... the day after I met you?

FRANK

Yeah. That math checks out.

CHARLOTTE

Glad you took your time getting to know me.

FRANK

Well, 12 hours wasn't gonna cut it, I needed the full 24.

They smile. Small beat.

CHARLOTTE

How come you never... *[told me or asked me out]*?

FRANK

'Cause you were _married_. To like the Greatest Guy in the World! So I resigned myself to having a Secret Crush, thinking I'd eventually get over it, even if everyone I went out with was a distant second. ...But no one ever came close. *(Small beat.)* Then after James... *[passed away]*... it was like you don't ask out someone whose husband just died, that's... In Bad Taste.

CHARLOTTE

I don't know. Worked for Richard III.

FRANK

Yeah, but he had that whole hump-thing goin' for him. Very sexy.

CHARLOTTE

And who doesn't love a good hump?

Charlotte winces at her "bad" joke. Frank smiles/chuckles.

FRANK

Anyway. Once you finally put yourself out there, you found that guy Mark...

CHARLOTTE

Who's clearly an asshole. *(Has an epiphany! Pulls out her phone)* _And_ getting dumped.... Right. Now.

> *She presses a button and holds the phone to her mouth doing the "talk to text" feature. Ding!*

CHARLOTTE
(into phone, with an edge)

Hey, Mark. I'm breaking up with you over this text because you are without a doubt the fakest, stupidest, least appealing man I've ever met who isn't 26 or a Slimeball-slash-Jackass... or both. Good luck at your next Open House. Jerk! *(Presses stop. Ding.)* And send. *(whoosh!)*

FRANK

Impressive.

CHARLOTTE
(looking at phone)

Yeah. Except Siri changed "Slimeball-slash-Jackass" to "Salmonella Jackals." But he'll get the gist of it. Anyway - you were saying...?

FRANK

Right, just that, you know. 'Cause of all the stuff that happened... I never got my chance at the plate.

CHARLOTTE
Man, you really like baseball.

FRANK
See, just as well - never woulda worked out between us.

CHARLOTTE
I don't know - sometimes opposites attract.

FRANK
True.

Small beat.

CHARLOTTE
So. What is it you like... about me?

FRANK
It might be faster to list the things I _don't_ like about you.

Charlotte smiles, embarrassed, but wants to know.

FRANK
(starts slow, sincere)
But okay, um You remember everyone's name - even if you've only met 'em once. It sounds small, but it's a big deal. Shows people you care - that you're listening to them. You love animals. You're a great mom. You don't take shit from anyone, but you're not an asshole either. *(picking up the pace)* You always tell the truth and expect everyone to do the same. You don't suffer fools. You're funny. You have a lovely singing voice. You never forget // people's birthdays—

CHARLOTTE
Wait, wait - when have you heard me sing?

FRANK
You hum at your desk. And then at that team-building
karaoke night a few years back with all the New York
branches, you sang something from *The Music Man,* I think?

CHARLOTTE
(smiling at the memory)
"Till There Was You."

FRANK
Right! Everyone's singing Top 40 crap or stupid 80's
nostalgia, then you hit 'em with this classy Broadway tune
I thought you were the coolest person I'd ever seen.

*Perhaps Charlotte hums or lightly sings a few
bars of the song here. Or not. Either way, there
is a brief silence before Charlotte says...*

CHARLOTTE
...That was our wedding song.

FRANK
You and James?

CHARLOTTE
Mm.

FRANK
Annnd you can see why I'm still single. I don't know enough
not to bring up your wedding song... *while I'm hitting on
you.*

Frank silently chastises himself.

CHARLOTTE
(sweetly) Is that what this is... you're hitting on me?

FRANK
If you have to ask, then clearly I'm battin' a thousand.

CHARLOTTE
More baseball metaphors.

FRANK
Shoot. Sorry. I told you: I'm terrible at this.

CHARLOTTE
No. You're knockin' it out of the park.

They edge toward each other... and <u>kiss</u>.

It's passionate and sweet.

But then Charlotte breaks it off.

CHARLOTTE
Sorry, I'm sorry.

FRANK
No, *I'm* sorry. Is this too fast? *(To himself)* Of course it is, you idiot, what's wrong with you?!

CHARLOTTE
No - it's a great idea. It was *my* idea! And I appreciate what you and Diane have been doing, pushing to get me out there—

FRANK

Diane was pushing. I was an innocent bystander.

CHARLOTTE

Frank.

FRANK

Okay. A _curious_ bystander. Waiting for whenever you were ready. But not pushing!

CHARLOTTE

I'm sorry. You may be ready. But I'm not sure if I am. And... you don't want to get involved. I'm a total mess.

FRANK

Are you kidding? I love messy! Messy clothes, messy people, _Lionel_ Messi! Messy's my favorite.

CHARLOTTE

You're sweet, but I just. I need more time.

FRANK

Hey, that's cool, yeah. Take - take all the time you need.

CHARLOTTE

Thanks. I'll see ya.

She exits.

FRANK
(calling after her)
And like we tell our clients: Don't settle. Your Forever Home is right around the corner!

Lights shift.

SCENE: GRIEF COUNSELOR

> *Charlotte sits on the sofa. The Grief Counselor*
> *sits across from her. (Still speaking with his*
> *Irish, Scottish or British accent.)*

GRIEF COUNSELOR
Wanna tell me what that was about?

CHARLOTTE
Aren't *you* the one with the degree in sappy brain science?

GRIEF COUNSELOR
Why don't we start by telling me what YOU think it was about?

CHARLOTTE
Ugh, such a therapist cop out! "I got no idea what's wrong with you Crazy Lady, so *you*
do the diagnosis for me."

GRIEF COUNSELOR
"Knowing yourself is the beginning of all wisdom." …
Aristotle.

CHARLOTTE
(laughs)
Aristotle? Are you sure? I thought those were lyrics from a Taylor Swift song!

GRIEF COUNSELOR
Okay, fine. I'll tell you what I think is going on.

CHARLOTTE
Finally! I mean -- what's the point of coming here if I gotta
do all the work?

GRIEF COUNSELOR
You _know_ what you need to do... you're just too scared to do
it.

CHARLOTTE
(laughing)
"I know but I'm scared?" _That's_ your big revelation?!?

GRIEF COUNSELOR
Don't believe me?

CHARLOTTE
Uh, not really. I mean if I knew what to do, then I'd do it.

GRIEF COUNSELOR
All right, I'll prove it. On the count of three, I want you to
tell me what you're really afraid of, but know deep down
you need to do. Ready?

CHARLOTTE	GRIEF COUNSELOR
Well, this is stupid.	One…

CHARLOTTE	GRIEF COUNSELOR
You're gonna feel pretty dumb when you see this doesn't work out.	Two…

GRIEF COUNSELOR
Three.

CHARLOTTE

I need to sell our house!

Beat. The Counselor nods.

CHARLOTTE

But I don't wanna sell the house. That place means
everything to me, it's... it was our Forever Home.

He drops his accent (and speaks like James).

GRIEF COUNSELOR

Some forevers don't last forever.

Charlotte looks at him, stunned.

CHARLOTTE

Wait - what happened to your charming accent? And also...
"Some forevers don't last forever?" That's like a fortune
cookie written through Google translate!

GRIEF COUNSELOR

(speaking with the accent again, and for the rest of the scene)
And. That's our time, I'm afraid.

*He stands and slowly makes his way behind the
sofa/chair where Charlotte sits.*

CHARLOTTE

No - it hasn't been an hour. I didn't hear the ding!

GRIEF COUNSELOR

I mean *our* time. This is the end of the road.

CHARLOTTE

Wh- wh- what does that mean?

GRIEF COUNSELOR

It means now that you know what to do... it's time for you to
admit what _this_ is.

CHARLOTTE

Seriously - do they teach you people to speak in _riddles?_ I
feel like I'm in a Dr. Seuss book!

> _He's now standing right behind Charlotte. They
> both look out over the audience._

GRIEF COUNSELOR

You need to admit... that I'm not real.

CHARLOTTE

I need to admit that you're not real??

GRIEF COUNSELOR

I'm in your head.

CHARLOTTE

...You're in my head.

> _The Counselor begins to slowly back up into the
> shadows / out of the room._

GRIEF COUNSELOR

You've never gone to a grief counselor, therefore you've
never actually dealt with your grief. You're just...

GRIEF COUNSELOR	CHARLOTTE
Telling myself what I want to hear.	Telling myself what I want to hear.

CHARLOTTE
(scoffs/chuckles)
Which is why I keep repeating everything you say because
it's really me saying it. Right? Is that it? Is that what I'm --
[doing?]

Charlotte turns around... The Counselor is gone!

*After a beat, the lights shift and Charlotte moves
into a pool of light.*

SCENE: DIVING INTO WORK

CHARLOTTE
Okay. So. You've been lying to yourself. For two and a half
years. That's fine. That's normal. Lots of people do that. So
to get back on track you just need to... do what normal
people do. Which is what, I have no idea -- *(looking up, a
cry to the Heavens)* WHAT DO NORMAL PEOPLE DO IN
THIS KIND OF SITUATION!?!

*Diane, Frank and James all pop their heads
around a wall.*

DIANE	JAMES
They work!	They work!

FRANK
(with a sassy snap)
…You better work, girl!

DIANE
(to Frank)
No, unh-uh, don't do that.

FRANK
Sorry, sorry.

Diane, James and Frank disappear again.

CHARLOTTE
Yes! They work. Thrust yourself into work, Charlotte! Be the best realtor you can be! Forget about James or Love or Happiness. Forget about singing, forget your dreams. *Work* is the American Dream.

> *Lights shift as Charlotte gets a wild-eyed look in her eye -- on a mission to sell these homes! But during the following montage of scenes, Charlotte will go from being full of vim and vigor... to being exhausted and depressed.*
>
> *The other actors remain on stage during this montage and help each other into and out of their quick changes. It should feel frenetic, improvised and a bit messy, as if they never really rehearsed it.*

CHARLOTTE
(full-saleswoman mode)
This delightfully charming three-bedroom, three-bath is just a hop-skip-and-a-jump from all the hot action downtown.

> *CHATTY HUSBAND 1 & 2 scamper into the light wearing fancy sunglasses, maybe one of them wears a chic men's scarf. They both have over-the-top German accents.*

CHATTY HUSBAND 1
O...M...G... This place is. Ah. Mah. Zing.

CHATTY HUSBAND 2
Like for real, Hans. I'm totally in love wit zis wood-burning fireplace.

CHATTY HUSBAND 1
And zis kitchen with ze sexy backsplash.

CHATTY HUSBAND 2
I love a sexy backsplash!

CHATTY HUSBAND 1
And did you see ze outdoor barn?

CHATTY HUSBAND 2
Of course I see ze outdoor barn!

CHATTY HUSBAND 1
And are you loving ze outdoor barn like I am loving ze outdoor barn?

CHATTY HUSBAND 2
Are you joking me right now?! We can have dinner parties _IN_ ze outdoor barn.

CHATTY HUSBAND 1
_SO_ many ways to entertain!

CHATTY HUSBAND 2
We love to entertain!

BOTH CHATTY HUSBANDS
(turning to Charlotte)
HOW MUCH ARE ZEY ASKING?!

*They scamper back up for a quick change as
Charlotte walks across the stage while saying...*

CHARLOTTE
(less enthusiastic, but trying hard)
A rustic fixer upper with lots of potential that's off the beaten
path... and priced to move.

*A RUSTIC COUPLE appears, speaking with
<u>Rural New England accents</u>, wearing bandanas
or something that feels farm-y.*

RUSTIC WIFE
Ah-up. Solid bones on this one, Father.

RUSTIC HUSBAND
Indeed, Mother. A finer home I reckon I've not seen since
aught-eight.

RUSTIC WIFE
When the crash made homes affordable again.

RUSTIC HUSBAND
Ah-up. The children can do their 'rithmatic lessons right here
in the kitchen.

RUSTIC WIFE
And the chicken coop can go out by that stone wall.

RUSTIC HUSBAND
And the children can pluck the chickens for dinner after their
homework.

RUSTIC WIFE
Indeed, pluckin' chickens builds character.

RUSTIC HUSBAND
Ah-up. 'Tis a fine home.

RUSTIC WIFE
A very fine home.

RUSTIC COUPLE
(turning to Charlotte)
HOW MUCH ARE THEY ASKING?!

*They scamper away (perhaps one of them gets pulled back downstage to play the next part) as an EXCITED YOUNG COUPLE enters; they talk like **California Gen-Zers**.*

CHARLOTTE
(tired but powering through)
A somewhat lonely loft space that needs lots TLC but could be a real diamond in the rough...?

EXCITED BOYFRIEND
Tiff, am I crazy or is this place a total buzz-kill?!

EXCITED GIRLFRIEND
Total buzz-kill, Zach! But like, also? In a weird way? It reminds me of my Grandma's house?

EXCITED BOYFRIEND
Ohhhhh, yeah. I can see it now. Grandmas have serious vintage vibes.

EXCITED GIRLFRIEND
No cap. And that like...? Totally slays.

EXCITED BOYFRIEND
Nostalgia is really in right now.

EXCITED GIRLFRIEND
It's like so retro it's outro? And then retro again.

EXCITED BOYFRIEND
That's genius, babe! You need to put that on a sustainable coffee mug and sell at the next Farmer's market.

EXCITED GIRLFRIEND
Totes, McGoats. *(vocal fry)* So liiiiiiiiiiike... are we doing this???

EXCITED BOYFRIEND
We are totes doing this!

EXCITED COUPLE
(turning to Charlotte)
HOW MUCH ARE THEY ASKING?!

The Couple scampers back to the other actor(s). They all seem to <u>not</u> know what's coming next, racing to put on various costume pieces.

CHARLOTTE
(exhausted and over it)
This is... I don't know... another stupid house?

Small beat. The actors look confused then they all look at Charlotte.

EVERYONE BUT CHARLOTTE
HOW MUCH ARE THEY ASKING?!

Lights go out on the other actors.

Alone again, Charlotte steps into a pool of light. She takes a breath.

CHARLOTTE
(sincere)

This complete mess of a home with abandonment issues, a mild Ambien addiction and PTSD from losing the love of her life doesn't know what she should do next. Even after thrusting herself into work and ignoring her best friend's calls and avoiding all contact with Frank and just feeling lost and confused and scared because if you're lucky enough to find Love once, there's no way you'll find it again since lightning never strikes the same place twice, and if it does it only causes lasting damage, constant headaches and comes with a sub-zero fridge to lock away those feelings, keeping them cold and distant, and incapable of being hurt again. And unless she gets a sign telling her otherwise, she is never letting go, never moving on, NEVER, EVER going on the market!

> *Lights slowly rise on James sitting at an outdoor table drinking coffee, a nice men's messenger style bag at his feet (maybe distressed leather).*
>
> *He's looking at an early model **flip phone**.*
>
> *Charlotte turns to see him sitting there, then smiles wistfully at the memory.*
>
> *After a beat, she puts her hair up in a ponytail and is handed a old tote bag, and a bottle of water by the actors playing Frank and Diane.*
>
> *They give her an encouraging smile then exit as Charlotte takes a steadying breath then steps to*

the edge of the light admiring James from afar.

FLASHBACK - 23 YEARS AGO

James presses a few buttons on the flip-phone.

JAMES
(scoffs then mutters)
...need an engineering degree just to set this thing up.

*Charlotte enters the space fully, looking
flustered -- life of a struggling artist.*

CHARLOTTE
Hey, hi - sorry I'm late. Are you James?

He stands and they shake hands.

JAMES
Yeah. Hi. You must be Charlotte.

CHARLOTTE
Yes. Nice to finally meet you.

JAMES
You, too - you, too. Please, have a seat.

He gestures to a chair for her. They sit.

CHARLOTTE
Ah! I see you got one of those fancy mobile phones.

JAMES
Oh yeah, it's for work since I'm never really in an office, but

Waste of money if you ask me. These things'll never take off. Can I get you something? Coffee, juice. Bloody Mary.

CHARLOTTE
Little early for me to hit the booze - plus I'm a total lightweight, so.

JAMES
Okay then. Cheap date.

CHARLOTTE
…Cheeky.

JAMES
Sorry. Sorry. I've been trying this new thing where I say what I'm really thinking... sometimes it bites me in the ass.

CHARLOTTE
I'm gonna leave the "ass biting" right where it is. Not touching that one.

JAMES
(smiling)
Probably a good idea. So, uh. Diane tells me you're a singer.

CHARLOTTE
Yeah, kind of. I mean. it doesn't pay the bills just yet. And if something doesn't catch on. soon I may have to go knocking on Diane's door for a job selling houses.

JAMES
Well, I build and renovate houses, so. If you _do_ ever sell them, I can give you leads on which ones are coming to market.

CHARLOTTE

I'll take it.

JAMES

And did Diane also say you were from Israel?

CHARLOTTE

Yeah, that's right.

JAMES

Huh. So how come you don't...?

CHARLOTTE
(thick Israeli accent)
How come I don't go around talking like this...? (normal) I
was actually born in Denmark, then we moved to Israel
when I was five - so since I spoke two languages fluently at
such a young age, I was able to learn English without an
accent.

JAMES

Wow, cool. So... were you in the army?

CHARLOTTE

Why is that every American's first question about growing
up in Israel?

JAMES

Because it's impressive.

CHARLOTTE

Not really.

JAMES

Being in the army isn't impressive?

CHARLOTTE

No. In Israel, it's just What You Do. It's what everyone does. It'd be like saying, *"Wow you went to <u>middle school</u>. Impressive."*

JAMES

Well - you're still more impressive than me.

CHARLOTTE

We'll see about that. So, other than building and renovating the best homes in town, what else do you do?

JAMES

Uh, not much. I read, I like running...

CHARLOTTE

You're right. Not impressed.

JAMES

See?! I told you - I'm completely boring.

CHARLOTTE

You're not boring - you're just falling into the First Date Trap.

JAMES

There's a First Date Trap?

CHARLOTTE

Yes! Everyone plays it safe. Talks about the routine stuff. But when you made that admittedly lame joke about me being a "cheap date," I thought: Okay! Not the best line in the world, but this guy's got potential to Not Be Boring.

JAMES

That's a pretty low bar.

CHARLOTTE

Come on - we all have something cool and unique about us.
What's yours?

James looks at her. Is she for real?

CHARLOTTE

This could be a typical first date where we hide who we
really are until date number seven --

JAMES

I like the idea of date number seven.

CHARLOTTE
(smiling)

Or. We break the mold. Throw caution to the wind. Expose
our true selves on day one. So... What's it gonna be, J?

JAMES

No one calls me "J."

CHARLOTTE

They do now.

He chuckles.

JAMES

...What am I gonna call you?

CHARLOTTE

Dealer's choice.

He thinks about it. Throws caution to the wind.

JAMES
... "C" would be too obvious, so... how about... <u>CC</u>.

CHARLOTTE
Oo, CC for Charlotte Cohn, I like it. Now tell me what's cool and unique about you... J.

JAMES
(chuckling)
Okay, so. There is this one thing. Actually two things... They're both dumb though. Totally embarrassing.

CHARLOTTE
Yes! It sounds perfect. Dish!

JAMES
I, uh. I have this digital camera--

CHARLOTTE
Ugh, so embarrassing!

JAMES
(smiling)
Funny. And, uh... for birthdays and holidays and stuff, I like making photo collages for people. I just send the pictures to this company and *they* put it all together in a big frame. But going through the old photos on my camera, picking out the best ones...? Makes me feel like I've spent time with the people I'm giving the gift to. And like maybe I'll get to be a small part of their lives forever... I don't know, I told you it was dumb.

CHARLOTTE

No, that's awesome. Photo collages are the best. *(James sort of nods, embarrassed.)*...What's the second thing?

JAMES

...Sometimes I... write poetry.

CHARLOTTE

Really.

JAMES

It's corny, I know.

CHARLOTTE

No, no - that's also really cool. I love poetry.

JAMES

No one really loves poetry. But I love *writing* it. And since I can't sing like you, or play an instrument or anything, I figured... Anyone Can Write. At least a little. So it scratches that creative itch we all have.

CHARLOTTE

...Are you gonna write a poem about this?

JAMES

This date?

CHARLOTTE

Mm.

JAMES

Depends on whether or not it works out.

CHARLOTTE

Heartbreak makes for good poems, too.

JAMES

That's what I mean. If we live happily ever after... then I
never have to write about it.

CHARLOTTE

Well. Here's hoping you never write a poem about us. But I
will take a photo collage one day.

JAMES

Ah! Speaking of which...

*James pulls out a **digital camera** from his bag.*
Charlotte laughs.

CHARLOTTE

What, now? No, I look terrible.

JAMES
(aiming the camera)
No. It's great. It's real, in the moment.

She blushes and sort of makes a funny but
charming pose. James snaps a picture.

JAMES

...Perfect.

Beat.

CHARLOTTE

Oh, man.

JAMES

What?

CHARLOTTE

...Are you gonna break my heart, J?

JAMES

Not if you break mine first, CC.

> *They size each other up. There's something here.*
> *They both sense it. And love it.*

CHARLOTTE

Maybe I will have that Bloody Mary.

JAMES

Yeah, I'll join you. (*turns to an unseen waiter*) Waiter!

> *Lights shift as <u>James freezes</u> with a hand in the*
> *air calling the waiter.*
>
> *Charlotte smiles and nods to herself. The*
> *memory helped her make this next decision.*
>
> *She stands and crosses downstage as the lights*
> *fade on James and...*

<u>SCENE: GIFTS FROM BEYOND</u>

> *Charlotte moves into a pool of light down center.*
> *She is emotional... finally letting go of a large*
> *piece of who she is: her home.*

CHARLOTTE

This classic mid-century home with a spacious backyard,
four bedrooms and a large walk- in closet off the primary
suite is the ideal place to raise your strong, emotionally
grounded daughter with the Love of Your Life... right up
until the day he dies.

(Pause.)

Perfect for a couple ready to make lasting memories. And
help the previous owner finally move on with her life
New to market.

> *Lights rise on a NICE COUPLE. They have
> adorable <u>Long Island accents</u>.*
>
> *The wife looks to be about <u>seven months
> pregnant</u>. She stands near Charlotte while the
> Husband pokes around the space.*

NICE WIFE

So you're the realtor *and* the seller? That's so cool. Honey,
don't you think that's so cool?

NICE HUSBAND
(not really listening)

Totally cool.

NICE WIFE

Does that happen a lot?

CHARLOTTE

Not often. But in this case, I wanted to be the seller because I
kind of... never mind, it's silly.

NICE WIFE

No, tell us!

CHARLOTTE

...This is the house where we raised our daughter. Got a dog, hosted our first family Thanksgiving, had movie nights, game nights, made the front yard look like a spooky Halloween "_Dead_ & Breakfast." And I wanted to make sure it got passed on to someone... Worthy   Does that make sense?

NICE WIFE

It makes. _Complete_ sense. Doesn't it, hon?

NICE HUSBAND
(still not listening)

Total sense.

NICE WIFE

So why are you moving? (_Leans in_) Is something wrong with the house? With two kids and a third on the way, I'm too tired for any _meshugas_, so just level with me - I can take it.

CHARLOTTE
(smiling)

Oh no, no. The house is... perfect. More than anyone could ask for. But. My husband passed away two and a half years ago —

NICE WIFE

Oh, I'm so sorry.

CHARLOTTE

Thank you. And our daughter goes to NYU so I wanted to be closer to her and... I needed a change. I'll still do _this_ (_gestures vaguely to "selling houses"_) just... in the city.

NICE WIFE

Well. Change is good. I always say, "If you're feeling too comfortable, it means you're stuck." Don't I always say that, babe?

> *The husband has been poking around and finds his way to an <u>electrical panel</u> that's painted to look like a little work of art.*

NICE HUSBAND

Totally says that. What's this?

CHARLOTTE

Oh - the electrical panel. I hate how they're always this ugly, gunmetal grey. So I had James, my uh, my husband, make it more festive.

NICE HUSBAND

Cool. Can I take a peek?

CHARLOTTE

Sure. The wiring is excellent throughout the house. James worked with all the best people in town, so. No worries there.

> *He pops open the panel to look at the fuse box.*

> *Once the little door opens, **<u>an envelope</u>** falls to the ground. (It had been hidden behind the panel door.)*

> *The husband picks up the envelope which has Charlotte's name written in lovely script on it.*

NICE WIFE

What's that, hon?

NICE HUSBAND

I dunno. It just fell out when I opened the... little door thingy.

NICE WIFE

You mean "the electrical panel?" He pretends like he's
handy, but really knows nothing about houses.

NICE HUSBAND

I know about houses.

NICE WIFE

// Oh really?

CHARLOTTE

Excuse me. Could I... could I see that?

NICE HUSBAND

Oh yeah, sorry, of course. Looks like a note for "Charlotte."

He hands it over.

NICE WIFE

Ooo. Isn't that *your* name?

Charlotte nods, staring at the envelope.

NICE WIFE

...Aren't you gonna open it?

CHARLOTTE

I don't know if I'm ready.

NICE HUSBAND
Ready? It's just an envelope.

CHARLOTTE
I know, but... I've been having trouble with envelopes lately.

Ding-dong. The doorbell rings.

The Husband & Wife turn to look at the door.
Charlotte doesn't flinch. They look back at
Charlotte.

NICE HUSBAND
How are you with doorbells?

Charlotte still doesn't move.

NICE WIFE
Honey, why don't you...?

NICE HUSBAND
Yep, be right back.

He goes to answer the door. The Wife stands
awkwardly as Charlotte continues to stare at the
envelope

NICE WIFE
...Ya know what I hate about envelopes? Licking the back to
seal 'em. Who ever thought that was a good idea? So gross.
Now I only buy the self-seal kind.

Charlotte still doesn't move.

NICE WIFE
(mutters, rubbing her belly)
…Tough room.

> *The Husband returns with a DHX DELIVERY*
> *GUY carrying <u>a package</u>. The Delivery Guy*
> *wears a red & yellow uniform and hat. He*
> *speaks with <u>a strong Long Island accent</u>.*

DELIVERY GUY
Whoa - full house here! All right - now do you any of you
fine people happen to be uh…*(reading label)* Charlotte
Cohn-Dennison?

CHARLOTTE
That's me.

DELIVERY GUY
Bada-bing! Now we're cookin' with gas. Got a delivery for
you, ma'am.

> *He hands her a digital clipboard to "sign" her*
> *name.*

DELIVERY GUY
Now first -- on behalf of everyone at DHX, I want to
apologize for the tardiness of this here delivery.

CHARLOTTE
Okay... How late is it?

DELIVERY GUY
Just shy of two and a half years.

NICE WIFE
Two and a half _years_?!

DELIVERY GUY
Twenty-nine months to be exact. Yes, ma'am.

CHARLOTTE
(light chuckle)
Of course.

Everyone else looks confused.

NICE HUSBAND
Who's it from?

DELIVERY GUY
(checking his paperwork)
Lemme see here... a Mr. James Dennison. Mm-hm.

CHARLOTTE
(stammering)
...Wh-- I mean how did-- what happened?

DELIVERY GUY
Well, we had an unfortunate situation a few years back. A
fella got to takin' his delivery truck to the beach every
morning to go _surfin'_ -- then ditchin' whatever packages he
didn't have time to deliver. *(Whispers conspiratorially)* I
think he was smokin' the reefer. *(Normal)* He was promptly
fired of course, but never said where the boxes were at.
Prolly so stoned he couldn't remember! Then about a month
ago, they discovered the missing packages in an abandoned
warehouse. We've been tryin' to get 'em to their rightful
owners ever since.

Speechless, Charlotte signs then hands back the

clipboard as he hands her the package.

NICE WIFE

That's incredible.

DELIVERY GUY

The world's a magical, mysterious place. Hey, you's have a great day now, all right?

> *He leaves with a wave, whistling or humming a happy tune as he exits. (Perhaps something like "Till There Was You.")*
>
> *Charlotte and the married couple watch as he exits; they are all stunned.*

NICE WIFE

...Have you ever in your life...?

NICE HUSBAND

Never.

NICE WIFE
(to Charlotte)

...Hey. Are you all right?

CHARLOTTE

Mm? Yeah. Why wouldn't I be? 'S totally normal thing: just got a delivery from my dead husband, so you know *(blows a raspberry)* no biggie.

NICE WIFE

...Aren't ya gonna open it?

> *Charlotte goes to open the package. But it's taped up.*

NICE HUSBAND

Oh, here - let me help with that.

> *He gets out the pocketknife on his keychain and helps her open the package.*

NICE WIFE

Psh. He's had that pocketknife on his keychain for three years just *dying* for an excuse to use it in front of me.

NICE HUSBAND

And today's your lucky day.

> *The husband makes a "manly" face at his wife who nudges him and smiles lovingly.*

> *Package open, Charlotte removes the item inside so the audience see it first: **a framed photo collage**, about 2 feet by 3 feet.*

> *Charlotte then turns the picture frame around and sees it for the first time. She stares at it, misty-eyed.*

NICE WIFE

What is it?

CHARLOTTE

A photo collage. Me on my first date with James... our honeymoon... Our daughter being born... learning to ride a bike... the three of us at the beach... all the way through his cancer treatments. He must've had this made a week or two before he died.

NICE HUSBAND

…Wow.

Small beat.

NICE WIFE
(swatting her husband on the arm)
How come you and the kids never make me one of those for
Mother's Day? *(To Charlotte)* They just get me Gift Cards
from Kohl's.

NICE HUSBAND
(quietly)

Honey.

NICE WIFE
Sorry, I overshare when stuff gets real.

*Small beat. The Wife places the envelope on a
countertop or table.*

NICE WIFE
…Well, we should probably get outta your hair.

CHARLOTTE
Actually, could you do me a favor and open that, too. *(Nods
to the envelope.)* Not sure I'm emotionally ready for what's
inside.

The Husband hesitates. The Wife steps in.

NICE WIFE
Yeah, of course we can. Right, honey?

*The Wife gives the envelope to her Husband as
Charlotte places the photo collage down and
tries to remain calm.*

*The Husband opens the envelope (maybe using
his trusty pocketknife again) and removes a
typed letter from inside.*

NICE HUSBAND

Looks like a letter written on an old-timey typewriter. *(light
chuckle)* Huh. Didn't know people still did that.

NICE WIFE
(excited claps)

Ooo! Read it, read it!

*He offers it to Charlotte to read. She lightly
shakes her head "no" but gestures for him to do
the honors. He shrugs.*

NICE HUSBAND
(reading)

"My darling, CC…"
(picks up head)
You sure it's okay // if I –

NICE WIFE   CHARLOTTE
Yes!   Yes!

NICE HUSBAND

Got it.
(back to reading)
*"My darling, CC…. I don't know when you're reading this,
but I'm guessing it's been long enough that you're ready to
sell the house and move. Some nosy buyer or electrician*

98

NICE HUSBAND (cont)
asked you to open the panel -- and you found this"
(picks up head)
But wait - what if there had been a power outage or you blew
a fuse before then?

NICE WIFE
(snaps at him)
Didn't she tell you, the wiring in this house is excellent!
Keep. Reading!

NICE HUSBAND
Okay, sheesh.
(reading)
"And I knew you wouldn't be ready to <u>move</u>..."

The lights shift as JAMES enters, already
talking. He crosses in front of the Husband. (The
Husband and Wife are suddenly in dim light).

James and Charlotte both face out as he recites
his letter from memory.

JAMES
"...until you were ready to <u>move on</u>. And ready to hear <u>this</u>:
We were each other's Forever.
But some forevers don't last forever.

Charlotte gives a knowing smile. This was the
fortune cookie wisdom from earlier.

JAMES

"Still, 20 years is a damn good run, if you ask me.
And now that our forever is over. It's time for you to find a
New Forever.
Or... maybe you have - maybe you're already shacking up
with some 28-year-old fitness instructor and this letter is
totally superfluous.

Charlotte laughs through tears.

JAMES

"Either way... know that all I want is for you to be happy.
For Imogen to be happy. For Pepper to get 3 walks a day
and stop puking in the car. But most of all... I want you to be
Okay Moving On.

I mean, don't forget me! I still want like a Shrine of Photos
all around whatever new house you buy. You can start with
that photo collage I had made!

But I also think it's possible to find Love more than once in
this life. You just have to be willing to let go... and let it find
you.
Plus - you're too good a catch to become the old single lady
wearing turquoise jewelry, walking her geriatric dog in a
stroller.

Charlotte smiles/laughs.

JAMES

"I'm sure this time has been difficult.
And I'm really glad it was me who went first, 'cause...
I don't know how I'd cope without you to talk to every day.

JAMES (cont)

To dance with in the living room when a fun song comes on TV,

to smack butts when we pass each other in the kitchen - just because,

to talk about our hopes and dreams and our beautiful little lady that we somehow managed not to completely screw up. Did she get into NYU, by the way? God, I hope so!

See... I can't help talking to you about all the little things, even when I'm gone.

And we can still talk about the little things, by the way. Just don't do it in public and you'll be okay.

> *James turns and faces Charlotte (she still faces out).*

JAMES

"And I think that's the real takeaway from this long rambling note, CC: No matter what you do next...
Everything Will Be Okay. I love you. Always.
J."

> *He steps to Charlotte. Kisses his own hand and places it on her cheek.*
>
> *Charlotte shudders. She felt it. It's magical and mysterious and lovely.*
>
> *The lights shift as James recedes into the shadows and the Nice Husband and Wife are in light again.*
>
> *The husband folds the letter, handing it and the envelope back to Charlotte. She takes it graciously.*

Small beat.

The Wife <u>blows her nose loudly</u>.

NICE WIFE
That was the most beautiful thing I've ever heard! ...Sorry.
Hormones!

*She sniffles a few more times. Her husband
comforts her. A nice beat.*

NICE HUSBAND
...We'll take it.

CHARLOTTE
...The house?

NICE HUSBAND
I don't wanna be presumptuous. I know you want it to
remain in good hands, but... we'd be honored to have this be
our Forever Home.

*He squeezes his wife's hand and they smile at
each other. Charlotte nods.*

CHARLOTTE
(smiling through tears)
...I'll send over the paperwork this afternoon.

*They all have a nice moment together, then the
couple leaves.*

NICE HUSBAND
(to his Wife, while exiting)
That really was beautiful.

NICE WIFE

I know! And then the delivery guy, with the thing! Uh! Gorgeous!!

Charlotte scans the letter again to herself, flips it over absent-mindedly and spots a postscript.

She looks at it closely then puffs out a laugh.

CHARLOTTE

... James, you sneaky bastard.

Lights shift.

SCENE: EVERYTHING WILL BE OKAY

Charlotte remains in her home holding the letter as Diane enters and begins pacing.

DIANE

This is weird.

CHARLOTTE

I know.

DIANE

Like *cosmically* weird.

CHARLOTTE

I know.

                              DIANE
                          (stops pacing)
I write a fake letter - and all this time there was an _actual_
letter from James hiding in your wall? _AND_ you get a photo
collage from him two and half years late?!

                            CHARLOTTE
Like you said: weird.

                              DIANE
                      (goes to grab the letter)
Can I read it again?

                            CHARLOTTE
Five times is plenty.

                    Diane raises her hands, "My bad." Small beat.

                              DIANE
You gonna tell Frank?

                            CHARLOTTE
I texted him this morning. Asked to meet up. He should be
here any minute.

                              DIANE
                  (gathering her purse and things)
Then I. Will get outta your hair.

                            CHARLOTTE
Got any big plans later?

                              DIANE
Actually. Steve and I are having a romantic date night.

CHARLOTTE
Fun! Going to your usual spot?

DIANE
No, we're, uh. Gonna try this new French place... in the _city_.

CHARLOTTE
Look at you, Fancy!

DIANE
I know, I know. Figured I should put my money where my
big mouth is. Work on my own love life.

> *Charlotte nods at her. They share a nice*
> *wordless moment. Diane starts off. Stops.*

DIANE
And _we're_ good, right? You and me? We don't need to do a
whole... apology thing.

CHARLOTTE
We are definitely good.

DIANE
I mean, you're like my sister. _Better_ than my sister because I
love you _and_ I like you.

CHARLOTTE
Back atcha, babe.

DIANE
(full of love and emotion)
Good. Glad we got that taken care of. 'Cause I don't know
what I'd do without you.

> *Diane breaks down crying. Charlotte hugs her.*

CHARLOTTE
Hey! Don't worry. Everything will be okay.

DIANE
(through weepy tears)
How do you know?!

CHARLOTTE
...The note said.

There's a light knock on the door. Charlotte and Diane break the hug as Frank enters.

FRANK
Hey, the door was open, so I -- (*sees Diane*) Oh. Is this a work thing?

DIANE
(quickly sniffing back tears)
No, Frank. This is very much *not* a work thing. But uh... if the two of you feel like calling in sick later...? I think that can be arranged....

She gives a suggestive look/smile/wink before exiting. Charlotte waves her off, embarrassed. Frank is confused.

FRANK
What's *her* deal?

CHARLOTTE
Enh. I think she's drunk.

FRANK

...It's not even 10 a.m.

CHARLOTTE

Then I don't know. Thanks for coming over.

FRANK

Yeah. Well. It sounded important.

CHARLOTTE

It is. I, um. Well, first I wanted to tell you that... I'm moving.
To the city. Gonna give singing another try.

FRANK

Really. *(Charlotte nods.)* Oh, wow - that's awesome,
Charlotte. I love that.

CHARLOTTE

Yeah, thanks. And also... I wanted to apologize.

FRANK

No, *I* should apologize --

CHARLOTTE

Wait. Lemme finish.

He demurs.

CHARLOTTE

For a long time... I felt like a piece of me was missing. And
no mater where I was, a small part of me was always looking
for that Missing Piece. And I've been afraid to either let go
of *looking* for it... or afraid to find a New One. Because I
wasn't sure who I'd *be* if I was whole again. But now. I think
I'm finally ready. To Be Whole.

FRANK

...Wow, that's. What changed your mind?

CHARLOTTE

My heart. I changed my heart and that changed my mind.
Also I found this.

She hands the letter to Frank.

FRANK

What's this?

CHARLOTTE

A letter. From James. That he actually wrote. You don't need
to read the whole thing now, but... there's a postscript you
should see. On the back.

*Frank looks at her curiously. Then he flips the
letter over and reads the P.S.*

FRANK
(reading)

*"P.S. I think you should give that guy Frank from your office
a shot."*

*Frank looks up at Charlotte. She nods and
gestures for him to keep reading.*

FRANK
(reading)

*"I'm pretty sure he always had a little crush on you. And he
seems like the kind of guy who'd look out for you, CC... and
make sure Everything Will Be Okay."* ...No. Is this a joke?
Did <u>you</u> write that?

CHARLOTTE

Nope.

FRANK

Diane, then.

CHARLOTTE

Hand to God - it's all James. He's the only one that ever called me "CC."

FRANK

...Sneaky bastard.

CHARLOTTE

That's what I said!

FRANK

Huh.

CHARLOTTE

And on that note... since I won't be in the neighborhood anymore... I wanted to give you this.

She hands him a small ticket.

FRANK
(light laugh)

A monthly LIRR pass.

CHARLOTTE

See, there's this contraption they have called the *train*?

FRANK

Ohhh, I've heard of it.

CHARLOTTE

Yeah, it takes people previously trapped on Long Island and lets them escape into Manhattan for culture, restaurants, all kinds of great stuff.

FRANK

Like meeting up with friends?

CHARLOTTE

Like meeting up with friends. And now you have no excuse. Free ride.

A nice beat.

FRANK

So what's next... for us?

CHARLOTTE

What's next is... we skip work and get some brunch. Maybe find a place with bottomless mimosas - and baseball on TV so you can finally explain the world's most boring game to me.

FRANK

It's not boring. Once you understand all the subtleties and nuances. It's like chess with home runs!

CHARLOTTE

If you're gonna sell me on baseball...? Don't compare it to chess.

FRANK

Noted.

They smile.

CHARLOTTE
Then after brunch... we take things slow.

FRANK
...I can do slow.

> *They have a nice moment (maybe a short, sweet kiss) before Frank exits and the lights shift.*

EPILOGUE

> *Charlotte moves down center and turns to us in a pool of light holding a new set of keys.*

CHARLOTTE
This pet-friendly, two-bedroom Greenwich Village stunner with hardwood floors, a romantic breakfast nook, and a Little Bit of Magic around every corner has been recently rented by a Not-So-Young Widow making a fresh start on her Second Act in Life. Just blocks from her daughter's dorm, it's also close to some of the best restaurants in the city - perfect for building a new and lasting relationship with an old friend-slash-new boyfriend. Which means _we_ [meaning the apartment and Charlotte] are officially...

> *She tosses the keys up in her hand and catches them with the same hand.*

CHARLOTTE
Off the Market.

> *Blackout.*

END OF PLAY